I GOTTA MAKE IT!!

by

Tamar T. Swapsy

www.rdtalleybooks.com

Las Vegas, Nevada

ISBN: 978-1-957294-09-4

R.D. Talley Books Publishing, LLC
4882 W. Lone Mountain Rd.
Las Vegas, Nevada 89130
www.rdtalleybooks.com

Dedication

"I Gotta Make It" is Babygirl's testimony of survival. I would first like to thank my heavenly father for allowing experience's to change my life. My entire family for not always seeing what I saw about someone else, reminding me to stick to whatever I believe is true. All my nieces, nephews, and three God-children. Peers from grammar to adulthood, who looked over me like angels. She is thankful for everyone in her life.

What ever you tell and instill in self may be the source of getting through in life!

I Gotta Make It! (Prologue)

*Things one person disvalues, another may value!

*Use what you value the most to make a difference in yourself.

*Encounters with angels are completely remarkable!

*Peace, Place, Process, and Purpose!

*Angels exist to serve God and to give and receive messages.

*The weirdest situations may turn into the greatest miracles!

*A positive message will lead to unthinkable outcomes!

*Words, actions and determination saves lives!

*Encouragement saves lives!

Contents

I GOTTA MAKE IT!

My name is Babygirl. A good man came into my life and saved me from killing myself. He was sent to do an amazing work for God (Elohyim and Allah) Almighty. Understand that one friend may have the same issues as the next, yet familiarity follows two strangers with identical testimonies; two strangers living in the same hometown of Kankakee, Illinois. One committed suicide, the other did not!

The stories may have occurred eleven years apart, but stories can repeat themselves. Lawrence E. Darling recognized signs of distress and made the choice to protect both of his peers. He did this by communicating and making suggesstions of ways to implement changes to assist with positive gestures for the safety of the ladies' well-beings. Also, he wanted to prevent from having to go to a second funeral. He went to one and became determined not to experience a second friend's death.

A young lady, before my time, experienced the same treatments from her family, just as I did. Patti committed suicide years before me. She spoke from beyond the grave. It was an odd experience, but it taught me a lot.

I believe spirits speak from beyond the grave, especially when one's life has been cut short to suicide and domestic violence within the family.

Patti asked me to do her a favor: "Thank Lawrence for what he has done in your life. He tried to do the same for me. I was just tired of fighting with my family. Seeing my skin change colors, the bruising, the cursing and the batteredness. Peers asking questions about everything and me making excuses for other's behavior. Please, thank him daily! You are the me that I wanted to be! I am the 'you' who wishes I was still alive! I thought suicide was the best and only option. I did not think of anything else. However, you thought of techniques to survive. It worked out for you! I wish I had your strength!" (Summer, 2018).

Praying, seeking guidance, silence, positivity, and encouraging words. I was unwilling to stay in a bad situation. Everyone was always wondering, "How did she make it?!"

Each and every time Lawrence and I spoke, I said my favorite phrase, **I Gotta Make It!"**, which brought comfort to every circumstance. Create strategies of healing for everyone who is monitoring everything. Silent lessons were taking place.

I think of Isaiah 64:8 and pray: *Father, I am your creation. Take me into your hands. Shape me and mold me as you will. I am your vessel. You shaped me with your hands for your purpose. May my life always reflect that I am your creation and bring you glory.*

The importance of sticking around when no one trusts anything, except the one looking in the mirror, is dynamic and never should be taken out of context. Listen to self's inner peace and thoughts regarding life and expectations of creating you.

"I GOTTA MAKE IT!" is a life lesson from changing bad to good while talking to self, never thinking twice of anyone observing the power in actions, behaviors, results, and words. Power resides in the tongue! *"There is that speaketh like the piercings of a sword: but the tongue of the wise is health."* (Proverbs 12:18, KJV). Healing occurs daily!

COMMUNICATION

Lawrence is 11 years, 7 months, and 17 days older than me. I was fifteen years old when we met, yet I enjoyed the company of older knowledgable gentlemen. It did not matter the age difference. What mattered most was the impact of conversations. Touching four hearts, minds, bodies, and souls: God, Lawrence, Patti, and mine's.

Clark Gas Station in Kankakee, Illinois represents peace, love, testimonies, prophesies, and experiences brought from all forms of angels. I was able to always reflect and be reminded of the love of words, hugs, smiles, visits, and willingness. It may no longer be in existence, but it remains the greatest memory within my heart.

Lawrence dreamed of Patti. He saw her and she explained, "I am back in a different form. Only you know it is me trying to make it." Then, Lawrence saw me in the dream within a blink of an eye. He immediately woke up in a cold sweat, puzzled by the dream of seeing an old friend he once tried to save from domestic violence. Patti understood the importance of sending a dream, even though she was no longer living.

Lawrence understood the objectives being to save my existence. I understood that I needed to keep showing up, dynamically changing bad from good, blessing one another by passing information for protection.

Once strangers, now Lawrence and I can talk about everything. I am blessed that two complete strangers could share a testimony; the gift of not knowing and knowing who is paying attention. *"Be not forgetful to entertain strangers: for thereby some have entertained angels unawares."* (Hebrews 13:2, KJV)

"Each of us should please our neighbors for their good, to build them up." (Romans 15:2, NIV). Every single time Lawrence spoke, God (Elohyim and Allah) spoke through him. He was a prophet in me and Patti's lives with God's messages in his heart. It means the world to both of us young ladies.

Finally, having someone who did not care about speaking up when both knew they could not do it themselves. Even though they abundantly tried, Patti and I have always been told that what they said did not matter. Therefore, both of us shut down and began different journeys. Lawrence taught us that our voices matter and we should use them.

Ecclesiastes 4:9-10 (NIV) states, *"Two are better than one, because they have a good return for their labor. If either of them falls down, one can help the other up. But pity anyone who falls and has no one to help them up."*

Proverbs 18:21 (KJV) states, *"Death and life are in the power of the tongue: and they that love it shall eat the fruit thereof."*

CHOICES

Don't ever do anything I am uncomfortable with doing. If I am not ready, do not let anyone pressure or force me, nor beat me down to do anything the way they see fit. Follow my own rules and guidance of the way I should live and how I want my life to turn out. **Some of the greatest lessons I've encountered!**

The family's unwillingness to listen to myself and Patti made it difficult to trust anyone, including ourselves. It is nothing but God (Elohyim and Allah) bringing changes by showing love through frustration and involvement. *"There is no fear in love; but perfect love castesth out fear: because fear hath torment. He that feareth is not made perfect in love."* (1 John 4:18, KJV)

The weirdest element of everything is Lawrence and I are still best friends. Likewise, the love has grown. No one understands, not even us. All he did was speak to me daily. As a matter of fact, he always reminds me, "I just spoke to you and helped you see what was going on was wrong!" I reminded him as well, "You spoke to my heart in a way of making me change myself." An unexpected miracle for two strangers, who now have an unbreakable bond.

"Love is patient, love is kind. It does not envy, it does not boast, it is not proud. It does not dishonor others, it is not self-seeking, it is not easily angered, it keeps no records of wrongs. Love does not delight in evil but rejoices with the truth. It always protects, always trusts, always hopes, always perseveres." (1 Corinthians 13:4-7, NIV). LOVE NEVER FAILS!

BEAUTY IS IN THE HEART, NOT THE APPEARANCE!

Experiencing beauty in the storm is the most peaceful attribute of caring. Forget how anyone looks; beauty is asking how someone is doing. Beauty is being concerned when not seeing someone. Beauty is checking-in. Beauty is love. Beauty is loyalty. Beauty is stopping damage. Beauty is silence. Beauty is loud. Beauty is acceptance. Beauty is recognizing. Beauty is heaven's words and messages. Beauty is in the hearts and conversations.

The undeniable heart is what matters most. Everyone always puts on make-up to look beautiful or try to hide past and present experiences. I have learned not to hide anything. I never knew how to apply make-up on my beautiful body.

People saw what they saw. Babygirl's concept of existence.

The Love of Conversations

The love of conversations will get anyone not to harm themselves, despite everything going on within any environments worldwide. Hearing and seeing family say one thing, which is built on nothing but lies, then hearing and seeing angels say the complete opposite is love.

Lies, love and lust: the three components of addressing elements of unrecognized and recognized behaviors. Warnings of conversations that go forth and allowing me to accept situations. Love of knowledge and power from all.

"May the Lord make you to increase and abound in love on toward another, an toward all men, even as we do toward you." (1 Thessalonians 3:12, KJV)

ADDRESSING ISSUES

1. "Babygirl, are you okay?" **I Gotta Make It!** (First time acknowledging things).
2. "Babygirl, huh? Black, does not always hide scars!" (Second acknowledgement).
3. "Babygirl, I love you with a great big smile!" "I love you, too!"
4. "Babygirl, your sisters and cousins came in here last night. After hearing all I have heard, I am going to tell it to you like this: only you can change everything! Do you know what was said when your sisters and cousins came to humilate you? Do you know you are being lied on? Your sister Daniella said, "The only reason why she does it is because one day, she over heard your mother (Tabitha) tell your step-father (Earl) say that he could do whatever you want to do to Babygirl! Just do not hurt the others!" (Third acknowledgment of things seen and heard).
5. "Babygirl, did you know?" "No, I didn't!" **"I Gotta Make It"** (Fourth acknowledgement).

6. "Babygirl, I had a friend who was exactly like you, except, she is dead (Patti). Her family treated her the same way your family is treating you now. It hurt me when she passed away. I do not want you to turn out like her. Her parents knew she was being lied on and targeted by her siblings, yet they chose to not do anything and ignored all of the warning signs. Now, she is gone. I regret not trying to do more for her!" He never gave a name (Fifth acknowledgement).

7. "Babygirl, I am not burying another friend because of domestic violence in their family!" (Sixth acknowledgment).

8. "Babygirl, you do not need anyone's permission to do and be you. Everybody is doing them! You need to do you! When will you?" (Seventh acknowledgement).

9. "**You Gotta Make Changes, Babygirl**!" "Thank You!"

10. "**Babygirl, please stop cursing!** It is unlady-like. I do not want you to end up with a man who is beating you up due to your mouth!" (Eighth acknowledgment).

11. "Babygirl, if you do decide to kill yourself, on the day of your funeral, I will give proof of everything you have experienced to your family!" (Ninth acknowledgement).

12. **"<u>Suicide is No Joke, Babygirl!</u>"** (Tenth Acknowledgement).
13. "Babygirl, my cousin sat in front of your house yesterday to show his son what could be done to him if he does not straighten up in life and school!"

Grateful for Every Message!

Understanding!

Clark Gas Station on Court Street was one of the components for saving my life. Family missed-out on the importance of conversations saving lives with peers who care, as well as the opportunity to build long-lasting foundations through communication and support.

Pursue your own itinerary in life. Yet, always remember, someone is constantly watching.

I tried to explain everything every time I was present. No one in the immediate family seemed to care. I learned not to listen to everything everyone had to say by the directions provided from the household. The biggest lesson I realized is family is not always right.

I *HATED* being at home, yet loved venturing out for peace of self and mind in school, working, walking, and vacationing. They presented opportunites to reflect, relax, and recreate everything.

If you have a **location** *which produces peace, go there! Stay awhile!*

Place

It is a blessing to have peers who only desires what is best for you, as well as your future. Traveling to Lawrence's place of business for spiritual healing and guidance gave me strength. Acknowledging conversations over the course of time, sneaking away to feel like I belonged in someone's life, confident of the outcomes.

At the age of 16, I was alerted of conversations my peers sustained with one another regarding all things seen. "Babygirl, your peers came into the gas station last night. Lawrence discussed everything going on from everyone looking in the windows! They saw and knew of the experiences you've encountered. Only you can change your situation by establishing transformations, beliefs and healings for the mindset."

My peers have been going to Lawrence's work place to have conversations of things seen, making the biggest differences of focusing on my welfare while looking through windows.

"I cannot believe she is going through it! Babygirl does not even do anything wrong to anyone. When she does get out, she will never be the same! No!

21

She will never come back! No! She is just going to leave if she makes it out. Whatever she does, it is better than living at home and putting up with domestic violence! Yeah!" (Spring, 1999).

The alert led to a decision of me not wanting to be around my immediate family as much as they desired. The same year, I stormed into Lawrence's place of work to declare change and victory. "Forget It! Forget It! Forget It! One day, I am going to leave and my family is not going to know what to do. I am tired of being the only one who is getting disciplined. I am tired of things only happening to me. I am just tired of it all."

"Lawrence, thank you for your kind words, love, and communication. If we never see each other again, please always remember this conversation. I love you, for everything!"

"I Love You Too, Babygirl! I am determined to change it all!" (Spring, 1999).

Tears of release began flowing from my face. Expressing emotions through crying is a sense of relief in my existence. *"You keep track of all of my sorrows. You have collected all of my tears in your bottle. You have recorded each on in your book!"* (Psalm 56:8-11, NLT)

PEACE

Lawrence is bold and never afraid to tell the truth. He learned and taught honesty, the best method of saving scarred and scorned peers. Stopping everything to have a conversation, conveying feelings of love with a smile, which will make anyone smile. I loved his boldness and willfulness to recognize issues in my life.

He pushed me to do, think, and become better, challenging my strengths within to accomplish goals. Alerting inner philosophies of every time anyone made comments concerning everything seen. Walking down streets or in the stores, visually seeing scars on the body. Determined, for no one to know all the facts, even wearing all black to hide everything, *so I thought.*

It only hid pain inside and outside of the heart, making everyone question whether Babygirl was Gothic or not? **<u>"Black does not always hide scars"</u>** is a true and powerful statement (Fall, 1998). It hides beauty and pain altogether.

Invisible scars reflect information the mind generates daily, rehearsing all the information replaying itself while lying in bed at night trying not to cry, asking God (Elohyim and Allah),

"Why is this happening to me?" He replied, "I will be a doctor, physician, and counselor in the time of need" (Psalms 37:39).

The visible pieces made everything unique and allowed self to say, "Enough of this bullshit! Leave and never come back." Issues seen and unseen, crippling from head to toe. No one sees me shutting down, quietness, shame, guilt, and frustration. I became so exhausted. No one sees tears, which counteracted the response of everything that has led to the decision, except me.

Being called jealous because my sisters experienced life much better than her. Everyone in the church and family thought I would be the first to get pregnant, even though I carry a secret that I will take to my grave in regards to protecting everyone.

I talk too much. The information is inaccurate and families are knowledgeable. However, they will never accept the truth of someone else's dishonesty.

I was aware of every time my sister Daniella would go up to his job to torment Lawrence about liking her sister, teasing him about her getting disciplined.

"Haha, my sister just got her ass beat because of my lies!" Everything Daniella said and did was pure gold in the family. She could do absolutely no wrong in their eyes.

Daniella stated, "My mother and Uncle Leonard will never believe anything that comes out of her mouth! They know I am lying and she still gets in trouble for my lies! Now, be my man or sleep with me!" Lawrence always replied, "Nope! I am at work and not interested!"

"Watch, I am going to tell another lie to get her in more trouble for no reason at all!" Daniella was so ruthless and deceitful. Our family was swift to believe Daniella and the crew quite often than myself. She got pleasure from seeing and hearing her sister get disciplined. She would tell lies, make up stories, and enjoy me getting hit. Daniella got in too deep with comfort of seeing me suffer. After a while, the crew seperated and Daniella was on her own.

The one sister who told the most lies and did the most harm asked me, "Why did you stop speaking?" I replied, "I did not want to be called a liar or worry about getting knocked to the floor anymore!" Daniella said, "Oh!", surprised, shocked, and amazed by the answer.

I would go months without speaking, almost an entire year of not saying a word. Only walking and taking care of business. It is healing for me. Everyone questions her reasons behind the decisions of not speaking. The next time I decided to speak, it made it hard for me to get the words out.

These are the reasons my sister stays away, unless it is concerning the children or peers I grew up with. Daniella was aware of my feelings of everything. Sometimes, she has issues with going back to Kankakee, Illinois. It is uncomfortable because of the lifestyle I lived. The first ten years of leaving and coming back, I developed issues with having flashbacks of the past. I'm now healed, better, and confident.

Mom was very over protective of all her children, especially me. She meant no harm; just tried to be there for my needs. Tabitha experienced an incident where the children next door were taken away and sent to foster care due to the mother's lack of care for their well-being and safety. Protection was the greatest vow Tabitha provided for her children out of love, respect, and circumstantial basis; to not lose custody of her Babygirl, worried until she decided to move to another state.

To start over with memories of Lawrence, her angel in her heart, mind, body, soul, and spirit.

TRUST

Lawrence brought his issues he was and is currently experiencing in his personal life. Searching for guidance on the best methods of handling situations. Trusting one another with secrets of two hearts delighting to do better. Sometimes, we are hard on one another and it does not last long. It is out of pure love, respect, and honesty.

Lies of always being blamed for other decisions in life. Betrayal of family, who had their cake and ate it too. Lack of trusting self.

"Do not believe, anything Babygirl says. She lies about everything!" Called a 'fucking liar' and 'weak' regularly.

<u>Blessed by Peers Staying Away</u>

"If anything happens to you and it does get reported, your peers will be to blame, not us!" This was a reason my peers never stuck around to get to know me. My mother's words haunted me at times. Nonetheless, it taught of the type of woman she desired to become: someone who is loyal, caring, compassionate, listening, and willing.

I was happy no one hardly came around. The circumstances created at home were not worth anyone coming around. I remembered a time when peers wanted to come over and color with me. Mom had me say, "No!" As soon as they left, my mother clowned me by saying, "You are not going anywhere. What you gonna do? Be a hoe when you go out with your peers?!"

"Mom, they just wanted to color with me!", I replied. I was disciplined afterwards and grounded for no reason.

I was always grounded for things I did not even do! I never fully comprehended the discipline given, yet it taught everything I needed to know. I refuse to sit still, even now.

I am grateful for everyone who saw, knew, and loved me, yet were told to not hang around me. Only care from a distance. I'm glad peers listened and paid attention, to their moms, dads, and legal guardians.

"Finally, brethren, whatever is true, whatever is honorable, whatever is right, whatever is pure, whatever is lovely, whatever is of good repute, if there is any excellence and if anything worthy of praise, dwell on these things." (Philippians 4:8, NASB)

Lawrence asked my sister Malka and cousin Roza, "What are they going to do if Babygirl does not want to be bothered? When the truth comes out? You are putting her through all of this! Does she even know what is going on? Does she know she is being lied on? All six of you! Malka, Laurel, Roza, Daniella, July, and Lex. What is going to happen when she finds out and does not want to be bothered at all? I am going to give you some advice: stop doing it to her, or else you will need her before she needs any of you!" I was overwhelmed with joy. Lawrence addressed the issues by speaking up for me. Roza and Malka made plans to not hang around as much.

"But speaking the truth in love, may grow up into him in all things, which is the head, even Christ: From whom the whole body fitly joined together and compacted by that which every joint supplieth, according to the effectual working in the measure of every part, maketh increase of the body unto the edifying of itself in love." (Ephesians 4:15-16, KJV)

He showed the man of God within himself by speaking the truth to everyone within the circle. A good man's steps are ordered by the Lord (Yehowah). (Psalm 37:23).

Family love generated feelings of consistency, devotion, discipline, and success. The love of family was rough, yet taught survival of living. I took it personally and was upset about things seen as well as heard. My mother (Tabitha) explained, "The way we raised you was not to hurt you, yet to teach tough love! You are strong in all areas of life. We plan to keep it that way. We do love you and want what is best for you!" The true love of a mother who has a disabled daughter with separate plans of existence.

I was not strong in all areas of existence. I just understood techniques of dealing with day-to-day negative and postitive interactions. I have walked down streets crying, laughing, smiling, screaming, and yelling to develop an understanding of myself. Even not being able to hardly walk and almost fainting. Nonetheless, having enough strength to go and see Lawrence to say, **"<u>I Am Okay! I Gotta Make It!</u>"**

A Four Letter Word To Some!

Love is coming from angels who acknowledge all. Love means listening and never judging. Love equals peace in the heart. Love is contagious. Love does not consist of dishonesty.

Lawrence began to grow fond of me and trusted me more as time progressed. He invited me to his grandmother's house to chill and relax. I had fear of being seen and disciplined in my heart. I wish I would have went to meet the matroic of the family when the first opportunity came. A man who wants any woman to meet their grandmother is a pheomonal woman. She will eventually trust her with her grandson.

I met his grandmother and it brought joy to both of us. As a matter of fact, I sat in church with Lawrence's mother (Ms. Royalty Darling) and grandmother. No one knows how much it meant to me to be unified with two beautiful generations of queens. Afterwards, I continued to visit while residing in Kankakee, Illinois. I became a free-will person and began visiting as much as possible. Ms. Royalty Darling was notified every time.

Lawrence even wanted me to meet his father, but each time, God (Elohyim and Allah) blocked it. He never understood why. Neither did I. However, the third time after not meeting his father, I got down on my knees to pray and asked, "Why is it being blocked for his father and I to meet? He is a man and I am a woman. Why, Heavenly Father?" The answer was interesting and quite fulfilling, from all walks of life.

Lawrence dealt with Karma by reminding her to not go after anyone who has their own demons they have to one day face in life. **"It is not Godly, Babygirl**! You do not want to be in trouble with the Almighty, based on a decision to try and get even. I am not having that out of you. I Love You, Babygirl!"

PROCESS

Lawrence's smile brightens the soul, heart, and room. I keep smiling, even when he is no where near. It is a memory of the heart and lives forever. God (Elohym and Allah) would pull us away from one another, working on both, teaching survival skills without being present, even though seeing one another walking down the streets of Kankakee, Illinois is always a blessing, especially when both of us worried about the safety of one another, even to this day.

No one and nothing could stop the reunion. Lawrence and I had not seen one another for months and worry began to set in. On the second day of summer school, I was walking and talking with a friend. The smile, walk, attitude, and saying my name. I tried to figure out the familiarity of knowing him. He called my name, "Babygirl!" Then, it clicked who he was. Nothing could stop the excitement of seeing him. Screaming his name while thinking of lost time and conversations, praying for the safety of each other, running with full excitement, love, trust, and missing one another. Unwilling to let one another go at the moment through accepting changes built over time.

Asking, "Where have you been? How are you? Why haven't I seen you?" Laughter filled the area and not wanting to let one another go while embracing with a hug. It was one we both still reminisce about. Lawrence explained, "I lost my job and started a new career!" My response was, "I was so worried about you and what happened to you!", trying not to cry and enjoying the moment. The conversation ended with their favorite words and smiles: "I Love You, Baby Boy! I Love You Too, Babygirl!"

ANGELS

Peers were concerned about not seeing or hearing from me, asking Roza and Laurel, "How is your cousin doing? Is she alright? We have not heard from or seen her in a while. How is everything?"

"My cousin is doing fine and I will tell her you asked about her." Stopping to check and see means understanding struggle is real. Caring for needs, wants, and desires of making sure I was still breathing and doing well.

Zila made sure her friend was in the right grade with her peers. I remember being in ninth grade, going to the table, and getting ready to sign up for an event or contest.

Zila asked, "What are you doing?"

"I am signing up for the event; I am in the ninth grade."

"No, you are in tenth grade with us and will be graduating with your class!" Zila knew her friend was a grade behind and did not care. She made sure she did not sign anything, yet also made sure I walked the stage with everyone.

She gave love by caring, speaking up, and acknowledging. (Spring, 1999).

Anastasia desired to see me go to prom in May of 2001 before graduating from high school. She stated, "I would have paid for you to go to prom. Why didn't you attend?" My response was, "I had to go to church!", with tears in my heart and eyes. I never had the opportunity to go. Instead, I went to church and was disciplined for asking if she could go to prom, forcing me to believe their way of living was better than hers. Also, to accept everything within my atmosphere.

All of my peers wanted to see me at prom to have fun with them and to experience a life of mingling and delight to the fullest. I learned what to do and what not to do in life. I am still content and goes out when I want to.

Peers and angels work hand-in-hand! Blessing those unwilling to say anything and acknowledging things seen. Lessons of seeing and communicating among themselves while expressing words of encoruagement. Valuing parents, friendships, loyalty, and respect. I appreciate everyone who went to talk about everything observed, whether in homes, gas stations, and every atmosphere in my hometown.

The desire to get out of the chaos, misery, and frustration of doing the same routines year after year, month after month, week after week, and day after day. Everyone in my circle at home and church always thought I talked too much. I hardly said anything to anyone.

My peers never judged the situation, yet helped by being compassionate, telling me to smile, laugh, and be apart of social clubs; forcing me to change the experiences and adjust to new adventures of thriving. Peers and angels function together to bring transformations to heal wounds.

THE ENGAGEMENT

Lawrence and Jackson met, however, they did not like each other immediately. They both expressed feelings of not liking one another to me. Jackson wanted me to leave Lawrence alone completely. He told my family and they tried to make me leave Lawrence alone. I said, "No!", then had a conversation about his reasons of why I should leave him alone. No one wanted to accept him behind closed doors. Lawrence was an angel sent from God to make changes and to save lives, while Jackson was an abuser sent to do harm; a difference between being treated right and wrong.

At the age of seventeen, I knew it was not going to last long. Jackson Pierce stated, "If I can be with you, I can be with anyone. I am not that interested in you anyway. I am interested in someone else who looks way better than you. Look at you with your scars! I am tired of looking at them!" (Spring, 2000). He set himself up for failure. The other young lady was never interested in him. Also, her family was not up for it. They protected her from him. (My scars are beauty!) I have learned to accept God's beauty and make the best of everything.

In the church, gentlemen always judged appearances rather than the heart of a virtuous woman. It taught me virtue and comfort; to be on a journey to not constantly search for Mr. Right. Anywhere! Anymore! Anytime!

"Let your moderation be known unto all men. The Lord is at hand. Be careful for nothing; but in every thing by prayer and supplication with thanksgiving let your requests be made known unto God. And the peace of God, which passeth all understanding, shall keep your hearts and minds through Christ Jesus. Finally, brethren, whatsoever things are true, whatsoever things are honest, whatsoever things are just, whatsoever things are pure, whatsoever things are lovely, whatsoever things are of good report; if there be any virtue, and if there be any praise, think on these things. Those things, which ye have both learned, received, heard, and seen in her. God of peace shall be with you. But I rejoiced in the Lord greatly, that now at the last your care of me hath flourished again; wherein ye were also careful, but ye lacked opportunity. Not that I speak in respect of want: for I have learned, in whatsoever state I am, therewith to be content" (Philipians 4:5-11, KJV).

Tradition is not always a good attribute. At the age of 17, I met a young man in church and was engaged a short time later. I was controlled by the tradition of seeing everyone get married, yet unhappy in the decision to marry. Sometimes it works and other times it does not. Make traditions that will not cost your happiness to be devoured. It truly is not worth the effort. Memories can never be changed, whether bad or good.

There were no records of healthy and long-lasting relationships, except two. It did not take me long to realize the set up for destruction. When he cried about the desire for me to leave him alone, his behavior behind closed doors was horrific. I experienced it. I was disciplined and told I was wrong about the decision to want to leave him alone, then made to stay with him. I prayed for a husband and got trash. I wished I would have never prayed.

I was engaged to Jackson in October of the same year, although I did not agree with the decision. He made about the future well-being of abiding by his rules and to leave Lawrence alone. Jackson was upset and didn't know any other way to express himself, according to him. I replied, "No! I will not leave him, alone!" He decided to raise his hand at me.

Never let anyone raise their hands at you.

Lawrence saw and addressed the situation by telling me, "Babygirl, I almost forgot I was at work and went to jail. I saw him raise his hand at you. You do not need anyone mistreating you and raising their hands at you! That is not love when a man raises his hand at you. The only thing that stopped me from whooping his behind was the fact that I was at work and behind the counter! Only you can change what is going on in your life! Please change it! I love you, Babygirl!"

"I love you too, Lawrence! Thank you!"

The second anyone in a relationship raises a hand at you, RUN! Never look back and wonder. Keep moving forward with the journey. Forget the comments from families, peers, and church members. They have shown you who they truly are. Recognize it as a blessing. Never go back to the scene!

I was extremely grateful Lawrence saw and addressed the domestic violence. I tried to inform my family about wanting to leave him alone. I was chewed-out completely by everyone in the church environment, forcing me to be in an uncomfortable and abusive position. The most damning part is the only reason that they wanted me to get married was so I would forget about my peers who made my life better. Not happening, at all!

Jackson and I never got married. I was grateful that a wise man, Uncle Leonard, stepped in to stop it. Pleased, he asked one question: "Why do you want to marry my niece?" Jackson stated, "I am only with your niece because I am attracted to someone else! If I can date your niece, then I can date anyone! I am not even interested in marrying your niece, just using her!" I was delighted he got involved and asked that question. Uncle Leonard stated, "Nope! You are not marrying my niece!"

He married his baby's mother on June 2, 2001, the same day we were supposed to have gotten married. On the wedding day, Jackson's brother begged me to intervene to stop the marriage. He recognized virtue in me, which was beautiful. This chapter ended and both of us were estatic about their decisions.

His brother asked, "Why won't you intervene? Come on, you know you want to! Please, if not for me, do it for him." I replied, "No! I am not that kind of a woman! I am happy he has found a wife." I was exultant his brother had found happiness.

She Survived Domestic Violence!

THE BLESSING OF GETTING OUT!

It was complete bullshit being engaged to him. Even being with him was a complete waste of time and energy. His heart and mind was never completely with me, nevertheless, someone who he never had a chance with. Thank God (Elohyim and Allah). I may have argued my way out, but it felt great to do so. I was extremely jovial for the both of them and excited to be left alone.

Honestly, I never loved him.

Afterwards, I was disloyal to family hook-ups in the church. Everything was about doing things their way or the high-way. My life was built around pleasing and making everyone else happy, but not myself.

Speaking of peers having a crush and wanting to date me, I was disciplined for speaking of non-church men dating me. It was pathetic. If family did not approve, it meant nothing to my family. I decided to not speak of young gentlemen anymore to anyone in my immediate family, teaching me self-diligence in choices to impact the well-being of growth.

"Do everything without grumbling or arguing, [15] so that you may become blameless and pure, "children of God without fault in a warped and crooked generation." Then you will shine among them like stars in the sky," (Philippians 2:14-15, NIV)

I remained single, celibate, and focused on graduating from college for eight years. Family were still trying to get involved with my love life and have me date who they desired. I always had a voice to say, "No!" Also, I moved out of Illinois for better opportunities and a better life.

Reflections

Visibility is critical! Reflecting times of good, bad, happy, and sad. Begging to be heard by someone, yet does not have the desire to believe anything. Picking up knives daily to end it all. Putting towels around my neck. Almost swallowing an entire bottles of pills. Pulling out clumps of hair due to stress brought on by others' plans. I dreamed of ways it would feel to handle everything differently, having faith of everything turning around in my favor one day.

Visible and non-visible experiences teaching motivation, adjusting to new ideas, concepts, and peace were difficult. It did not matter who did or did not agree. All that mattered were the lessons from one to another. All the adventures, experiences, love, and testimonies, even at the most unusual times and places in life.

Non-visibility reveals the turn-around of behavioral issues from domestic violence: developing a hardened heart, lashing-out at others and not seeing good in anything. It affects old and new relationships. Yet, it helps having someone contribute time of restorative tastics to realize some things can be changed and others cannot.

Building bonds that no one, except God (Elohyim), can hinder. Location does not matter. Developing opportunities of reflecting on good times. Meeting parents who are confused about everything and questioning, "Why are you friends with my son and/or daughter?"

For Lawrence, the purpose of everything is to change experiences, show love and show gratitude to avoid burying another friend. All resources come together to bring confidence to lives around the world. Sometimes, listening and understanding strength is not meant to be heard, only seen in the eyes of a few, not many, every step of the way in life.

Warning of things heard, seen, and encountered. Purpose to challenge interactions, discussions, and morals. No one willing to understand how in the world she has the capability of being disciplined, then going to have a conversation with an angel.

Never realizing how many peers were watching everything, observing in silence in one way or another. Speaking up to stop the injustice occurring to prevent harm when it is time for someone to speak. Healing the inside and outside of domestic violence is accurate.

Never going back to the place once known as home, making sure to never blame anyone within the circle.

Every day, I searched for and desired change, as well as a healthy environment and family. I knew they loved me, yet did not like those I liked. It did not matter. Each and every individual, rather man or woman, had God's agenda in mind: to assist, protect, and guide my life.

WORRY

Every time I did not see him or hear from him, I felt as if I did something wrong. I was completely wrong about everything. Lawrence was getting his life together for himself, his mother, grandmother and me to better his future and get himself in order. It made both of us proud. Unity was taking place and happiness counteracted. I had no idea until he sat me down and explained everything.

Even though we both talked about one another to our peers and family members, we received different reactions for different reasons. My family did not like my decision to stick by his side, yet Lawrence's family was happy with God's progress.

Reaching out to Roza about my feelings gave me the strength to not give up. I was told, "If you knew what I knew, you would not give up on him. Trust me!" Roza spoke in an aggressive tone. She knew things I did not. Roza was present when conversations took place. The smartest thing I did was listen to someone who knew more. She was never going to give up on God's progress while getting to recognize a great man.

Whatever anyone sees in another individual is what is kept in their hearts.

I always stayed busy in college and Lawrence always stayed busy with construction. Both of us pushed the other to do and become better for the happiness of self. I remember calling his house and leaving a message about graduating with a Bachelor's degree. Lawrence was very proud of my achievements and reminded me of my words. "Babygirl, you always said, 'I Gotta Make It!'" I was proud of him too.

Lawrence expressed feelings of wanting to go back to school and start classes. I was proud to hear his desires to attend school, yet he was kind-of afraid to go back. I was not having that. I did not believe in fear of any kind. I asked, "So you desire to do better and go back to school, correct?"

"Yes I do, Babygirl!"

I marched him in the kitchen with his virtuous mother, Ms. Royalty Darling, to declare he was heading back to school. I told her, "Your son desires to go back to school! He has three to six months to do just that. I will make it three months. If he does not, please feel free to contact me!" His mother looked at me and said, "Okay", in shock that I was making demands for his future happiness.

Lawrence went back to school in two months and told his mother, "Momma, I am doing this for you and Babygirl!"

Lawrence and I crowned each another with love and knowledge daily. Love filled the room while angels ascended and descended, agreeing in heaven and earth of the bond that only God (Elohyim) could break. The bond was never broken, only tampered with for 23 years. God (Elohyim) put two strangers together for him to get the joy. It takes only a few peers to see greatness in someone else.

Everyone who spoke, rather to me or behind closed doors, were angels of the Almighty God. Much of my strength subsides from environments of peers who made sure my life would be phenomonal; always asking questions, checking-in to see progress and expecting great answers. Anyone who has encounters with angels is blessed beyond recognition. It can be from a conversation, being pulled out the line of fire, lies, and love. The situation does not matter; the outcome of the testimony matter's most. God will send the right individuals when He is ready.

Everyone who speaks up regarding things wrong in someone's life are angels. No one knows when change is going to occur. The man above knew what he was doing when he sent his angels in me and Patti's midst. Powerful attributes derived from both of our testimonies and many lessons have been experienced. Two young ladies with the same testimonies with different outcomes. Rest in peace, Patti!

Decisions made led to failure and success, yet long lasting and unforgetable friendships. Think back to a time when someone made the choice to not see a friend fail. Blessings flowing with God's (Elohyim's) favor are meant to allow survival. Be thankful for everyone who takes time to speak for no reason. Angels are doing a magnificent work.

Negative opinions can and will harm everything around you. Negative opinions kill dreams. Negative opinions are trash. Negative opinions are wasteful. Negative opinions are not encouraging. Negative opinions are headaches. Negative opinions do not bring peace. Negative opinions, get them out of here! Stop listening when someone voices how they think the situation will turn out! Motivate yourself to see greatness in struggle!

On the other hand, positive opinions are everlasting. Positive opinions have endurance to heal. Positive opinions help to transform lives to build. Positive opinions do not self-sacrifice one's characteristics!

NEVER

- Never allow yourself to suffer to see another individual or family member happy.
- Never listen to one-sided details.
- Never believe only a piece of the information.
- Never believe only what you want to.
- Never be too afraid to engage in new activities with peers.
- Never be afraid to go with peers to meet their loved ones.
- Never discredit yourself.
- Never believe the way someone else wants you too.
- Never think that no one isn't listening.

ALWAYS

- Always be aware of everything.
- Always listen to yourself.
- Always be aware that someone is always watching.
- Always speak up!

Reflection

- Where would she be?
- How would it have turned out?
- What would life had been?
- Why didn't she?
- Who would peers and families be?

Thank you to all the angels who spoke & acknowledged!